Praise for The Mussolini Diaries

Gary Fincke's The Mussolini Diaries is a masterful collection of poems, particularly relevant for these difficult times, but like all great poetry, timeless in its own way. Fincke drills home what so many of us feel about the current state of our country with sharp insights grounded in complex imagery and spiced with wit and anger, empathy and loss. You too may find yourself nodding as you read, thinking, "yes, yes, this is how it is."

—Jim Daniels

With an unflinching gaze, Gary Fincke's The Mussolini Diaries grapples with our collective failure at good stewardship—of our planet, ourselves, and each other "…as if ruin were a handsome prince." In poems with themes as disparate as trepanning, climate change, suicide bombers, pandemics, clever forgeries, or the theft of one hundred brains from a hospital lab, our iniquities are laid bare and we are refused easy answers or hollow consolation. But Fincke adamantly eschews condemnation. In work by turns solemn and humorous, he manages to master a seemingly impossible paradox: despite the knowledge that "the world ripens without us…and we are sorely unmissed," though "we carry the memory of comfort like a congenital hump," there is still a chance at ultimate redemption where our "futures will have beauty and flight." These are timely, necessary poems that reward our reading and richly deserve our closest attention.

—Frank Paino

Praise for earlier books by Gary Fincke:

Gary Fincke brings a penetrating gaze and an elegiac tenderness to the telling "news items" he discovers in a world haunted by intimations of mortality.

—Chana Bloch

I am moved by how deeply these poems engage working class experiences, the intersection between the personal and the historical, the flawed, overlooked and often forgotten side of our daily realm . . . a book to be remembered.

—Edward Hirsch

The Mussolini Diaries

Gary Fincke

SERVING HOUSE BOOKS

The Mussolini Diaries

Copyright © 2020 by Gary Fincke

All Rights Reserved

Published by Serving House Books

Copenhagen, Denmark and South Orange, NJ

www.servinghousebooks.com

ISBN: 978-1-947175-29-7

Library of Congress Control Number: 2020938404

No part of this book may be used or reproduced in any manner whatsoever without the prior written permission of the copyright holder except for brief quotations in critical articles or reviews.

Member of The Independent Book Publishers Association

First Serving House Books Edition 2020

Cover Photograph: Jorgo Photography, 8 Queen Street, Zeehan, TAS, Australia, 7469

Serving House Books Logo: Barry Lereng Wilmont

This is with love to Derek, Shannon, Aaron, Gavin, Raea, Sabina, River, Doug and, as always, especially for Liz.

Table of Contents

Fimbulwinter	9
1	
After the Election, Traditional Forms	13
Symmetry	14
Isolation	15
Los Angeles, February, 2020: The Palm Pruner Explains His Work	17
The Beheaded	18
Drought-Struck Plants Squeal in Distress	20
The Past Tense of the Census	22
Open Carry	24
While our Newspapers Starved	26
The Instability of Stone	27
Limits	30
Fly Fishing, Parsing, the Faculty Retreat	31
In the Era of Collective Thought	33
Pentecostal	35
Sparklers	37
After the Election News, Human Subjects	39
2	
Contagious	43
The Mussolini Diaries	54
3	
The Election Remembers the Challenger	61
The Substitute Teacher Explains Climate	63
The Magician's Son	64
Carp are Dying of Herpes in Babylon	66
The Anxiety of Dams	68
How to Survive the Pandemic	70
Perspective	73
Soeur Sourire and the Vanishing of Nuns	76
The Importance of Captions	79
The Nocturnal Age	81

The Drownings of W. C. Fields	84
How Silly Grew	86
The Museum of American Tragedy	88
Solitude	90
The Director	92
Consolation	97
Hole in the Head: A Love Poem	99
On the Eve of the Presidential Election	103
Faith	105
The Invention of Worship	111
Acknowledgements	113
About the Author	115

Fimbulwinter

When the polar bears come inland,
the sea ice thinned to insufficient
for their thick, white weight, we close
our schools and lock our children in
to keep them, for now, from harm.
Outside, the bears wander, dozens
as confused as our sons and daughters.
Winter, it seems, no longer lives here,
but no one has taught us where to go.

The sea, undressed, is not ashamed.
Our children churn their chilly rooms,
stir our houses until each one softens.
Each morning we wait for winter
to recover. The bears' breath clouds
our streets. Their pacing splashes mud
across their heavy thighs. Nothing lives
north of our village; we must not tell
our children that all of us are seals.

When rain continues, we marvel
how prophecy has deceived us.
This end is being preceded by
a succession of modest winters—
last year's, the year before, now this.
Yes, summer will vanish, but into
this constant, twilit season conceived
by gods we have never understood
until, surely, the long-promised wars
that bear them witness will begin.

1

After the Election, Traditional Forms

My students are writing prayers, following
The forms of the ancients who expected
To be heard by more than eavesdroppers or
Family. Now they are considering
Their souls instead of marking their absence.
Doubt has drifted away from the table.
Mockery has left the room. Their ghazals
Contain refrains with Lord; their villanelles
Repeat: Resurrection brings white roses.
One writes a sequence of humility
In the metered lines of acquiescence.
Two finish devotion sonnets, saddened
By elections, afraid of those who hate
Aloud. On campus, they chant rhymed couplets
Of promises and march to the cadence
Of refugees. They hold their weeping signs
As if they were infants, wailing, at last,
The familiar litanies of longing,
The hallelujahs for their martyred hopes.

Symmetry

A boy wearing a tie he has knotted
Perfectly on the seventh try listens
To his grandfather explain how there are
Caterpillars who consume exactly
One leaf before they spin themselves to change.

Don't worry, the grandfather says, the leaf
Is large, but the caterpillar must feed
Carefully to keep the shrinking surface
So symmetrical it seems undamaged
When seen from the sky by birds who target
Food by the irregularity of leaves.

Even for the simplest minds, it's never
Enough to be camouflaged by color.
Remember those careful worms outsmarting
Their predators. How, without proof, they sense
That their futures will have beauty and flight.

The boy? He twists his tie, stifles the sigh
Prompted by Sunday instruction, but now
Grandfather says, pay attention, there's more.
Plants are always listening, and they know
The differences among the vibrations
Caused by chewing, the wind, and the harmless

Disturbances of insects. Detecting
The work of caterpillars, they let loose
A surge of mustard oil that ruins
Their appetites, driving those predators
Elsewhere, leaving astonishment to us.

Isolation

A day without news. Left behind,
last night's lead story -- a friend's
untimely death, his son surviving
the head-on two miles from home.
This evening, my near-misses
an embarrassment of luck
inherited like wealth. Three times,
after our father died, my sister
sent half of his years-hidden stash
of bonds, CDs, or even cash
that was never enough for news.
My friend believed the news was
a woman so beautiful he would
never tire of her body.
It was like his love of drinking,
returning daily to that desire,
sometimes seeking my company
for an evening that extended
toward the blackout of any sort
of news. Maybe that need
is a form of loneliness
that catches in the throat
like a concealed confession
for the disquiet of restraint,
a moment when we are, at least,
in understanding's vicinity.
Outside, three steep miles of trail
descend through forest. Apprehensive,
who wouldn't reminisce for comfort?
At 20:45, April 18, 1930,
the Wagner on the BBC,
as scheduled, was interrupted
for fifteen minutes of news.

Those listening to the radio
were worried, most likely, about
financial affairs, the way the world
was teetering toward another war,
but they heard "There is no news,"
and a piano began to play
as if nothing outside of their lives
had happened, and they could speak
to each other softly as the piano
continued, their living rooms
the extent of what mattered enough
to record and repeat, something
like the somber music after
Kennedy's assassination, each station
suddenly gone to cathedral organs,
bagpipes, and military bands,
all the instrumental ways
to indicate the news of loss
in the interlude between death
and its details through the static
of a distant station or the hum
that lives between frequencies.
In 1930, in radio's community,
every listener was intent upon
the first sign of interruption,
importance loitering outside,
even as the Wagner returned,
an aria at 21:00 without
the solace of excuses, one
by one shifting in their chairs
and beginning to whisper
as a woman cried beautifully
in song about unrequited desire.

Los Angeles, February, 2020: The Palm Pruner Explains his Work

First, he tells us, sterilize every tool. Soak them in bleach mixed one to three with water.

"Soak" means five minutes minimum. To sterilize the chain saw, remove the chain and bar and immerse both pieces. The same goes for the hand saw and knife. Rinse them with water. Air dry.

Climbing the tallest palms means learning to use a harness and cables. Spiked shoes should never be used. They will permanently damage the trunk.

Use the chainsaw for the large fronds, but care needs to be taken. Saw them close to the trunk, but do not cut the trunk. Cuts never heal. They will leave the tree defenseless.

Pull the boots by hand. Never attempt to saw them off. If they do not pull easily, leave them.

Do not use the tools on another palm tree without disinfecting. Never forget that diseases are easily spread by dirty cleaning tools. Where we are, fusarium wilt is the most likely. The lower fronds turn yellow, wilt and die. The upper leaves rapidly follow. At last, a few surviving fronds will form a spike at the top of the tree, but by now the entire plant is dying.

Remember, once a tree is infected, there is no cure.

If you somehow cause a tree to die, if you give disease its opportunity, you can replant, but understand that you cannot, though it tempts you with nostalgia, reuse the familiar spot where the old tree stood. Listen, even if that already softened and open area invites you, what killed the tree will linger there, patient.

Ignoring this advice is unforgivable.

The Beheaded

More than one scientist claims there was time
Before the Big Bang, citing evidence
That shrinks the cheap shirts of our lives until
Our bellies are revealed like perversions.
It's enough to reconsider the time
Before the Big Bang of our conceptions,
The world at ease with our absence, taking
Its ordinary time through the eons,
None of them ending in apocalypse,
No one rising from graves but characters
In stories, and yet I'm thinking about
The brutal contractions of loneliness,
Its extraordinary, unheard screaming
Before the wailing of what's become us.

A student, recently insisted we
Would recognize our beheaded bodies
As long as forty seconds, sufficient
For understanding. An insomniac,
She tells me she can see her sleepless self
The way the beheaded watch their bodies.
Such sight comes with wakefulness, she explained,
Her body prone for hours like a patient
Etherized, yet awake, one more story
I have read, someone hearing surgeons speak
The soft, private language of hopelessness.

Or this common story, my father's place,
This afternoon, among the nearly dead
In a room with a door that doesn't lock.
He is wrapped in flannel shirt and sweaters,
All buttoned to the throat while the heat hums
From every baseboard as he takes his pulse

Each hour, expecting to hear, I'm sure,
The incredible first silence of stopped.
I wheel him to the window he purchased
Thirteen years ago, the stained-glass mural
For my mother nearly two decades dead,
And he recognizes nothing until
I set him inches from her name and his,
Saying "read every word" like a teacher,
Already looking back on my visit
As it topples headless into the past.

How the world ripens without us, how mouths
Welcome its beauty and we are sorely
Unmissed, becoming spirit or nothing
But a generation's occasional
Remembering. And yet we are able
To answer annihilation with names
That science hasn't slaughtered; not yet, not
If we refuse to relinquish the love
That extends our moments by embracing.

Drought-struck Plants Squeal in Distress

The afternoons are worst, even
the succulents in the shade
beginning to whine like our dog
during its throes of dreams.
Those in full sun—the hardy,
decorative grasses, the iris,
and the prolific yucca--
drive us indoors with their
wailed cantatas of sorrow.
Months now, since anxiety
swelled to anger, how tired
they were of us explaining
that our surreptitious
dawn and dusk sprinklings
were the best we could do.
Look, we say, somebody
has cut our garden hoses.
Green is taboo, your leaves
a loud, public confession.
A short walk from here, fields
of corn cry in unison,
inconsolable as infants
in the expanding famine zone,
the ones whose mouths we used
to cover with monthly checks.
The house plants, though locked
inside their gated community,
are frightened by conservation.
For weeks, they have asked
for increased security.
Among themselves, they discuss
who would be easiest for us
to sacrifice, their squeals,

like yours, no longer coded.
Despite our care, even the cacti
loathe us enough to wish us
dead. Suicidal, they agree,
but the world, in time,
would flourish without us,
that assurance no more flimsy
than your cautious talk of souls.

The Past Tense of the Census

In the census year, with three small children,
My wife sought part-time work, self-designed hours
Convincing her to canvas our county
Of farms and quiet, well-zoned streets. There were
Heads to count, assessment questions, and not
Every house, she soon learned, was welcoming.
House trailers were rare and always alone,
Set so often on barely landscaped lots
That she was surprised, this late afternoon,
By one site's borders of high wooden fence,
A lawn weed-infested, yet closely mown
By somebody, she thought, who was taking
Whatever care he could, not a man who
Opened his door and stood naked to show
Whatever news he might possess could wait.

Once exposed, a man might be capable
Of anything, logic that hurried her
To our car where she turned, keys posed to thrust,
And saw the trailer door closed, driving home
Touched only by a familiar story
During the year Jimmy Carter looked sad,
As if he understood another sort
Of census would defeat him—hostages
Held in Iran, inflation, scarcity
Of oil--though we spoke nothing of that
While our children scattered around our fenced-
In back yard, twilight settling, our neighbor's
Black Lab barking longingly at the gate
As my wife began, hushed and intimate,
To speak while we stood beside the deck rail
So our children could see we were watching.

What did he say? I asked. *He was soundless.*

What did he do? He picked his teeth and spit.
How close was he? Arms' length. Able to reach.
I'm never counting him--is that a crime?
And right there her story ended as if
She was willing to tear only one page
From her notebook of murmured memory.

Carter is smiling now, benign with age.
Though he must have more than such small horrors
To tell, the country exposed and ugly,
Taken hostage and held for limitless
Ransom. That man, years ago, was surely
Naked as he watched my wife, a stranger,
Cross his cropped-weed yard. And surely, he had
His chance to choose shorts and shirtless or call
Out "Just a moment" before fully clothed,
Choosing, instead, full-frontal exposure.
That evening, all we could see of our three
Children was movement. They appeared to be
Vanishing, about to no longer live
In our house, my wife using the past tense
Of the census to say, "He was, he was"
In a sentence stuttering, then gone dark.

Open Carry

> *A Times Square crowd broke and bolted following a car's backfire*
> —News Item

Yesterday, at our local grocery,
my wife pointed out three
open-carrier families, the armed

walking beside small children
who squabbled over whose
turn it was to push bright red

future-customer shopping carts.
Our neighborhood, last night,
peered from darkened windows

at the sound of knocking going
door-to-door after nine p.m.
Text messages lit our bedroom,

uneasy flurried to fear
like a forecasted winter storm
until all of us were overheard.

Tomorrow, my daughter will return
to the church where her art school
for children, four to fourteen, is housed

two blocks from last weekend's
mass shooting. This week, she says,
the mediums will be water color

and acrylic painting, projects
arranged by age and experience
There will be scatterings of queries

about security. Some mothers will
notice the homeless served lunch
by the parish, a father will ask

who controls the AA meeting
held inside a downstairs room,
whether she has considered

locations dedicated exclusively to art,
or, at least, her plan for emergencies,
the details of the lockdown drills

she will ask his daughters to master,
testing, as he speaks, the strength
of the door, the challenge of its lock.

While our Newspapers Starved

During the endless war, the civil one
when we raised hate like hybrid tomatoes
our children could swallow like caplets,
our devices hummed like lovers' demands.

They glowed with memes. Their slogans walked
with us while our newspapers starved until
they became a few paragraphs, then less,
then merely a provocative headline with photos.

We open-carried at the grocery store.
We flew flags and sanctimony, trained
our dogs to be fences along the borders
of our small, carefully surveyed lots.

News kept breaking while we posted
the recipes of neighbors. Each update
sentence about the war drew thousands
of comments, punditry spreading

like highly contagious airborne flu.
Subtlety was shed like unwanted fat.
The world we knew was thinner now,
relying upon the app for true or false.

Each night arrived despite the debate
on darkness, whether or not it was
deepening, threatening to become
perpetual, expanding like a universe

that will never cease to widen, or,
according to others, collapsing back
into the tiny, pulsing dot that contains
everything all of us supposed was true.

The Instability of Stone

> "When the site of Christ's tomb fails, the failure will not be a slow process, but catastrophic."
> —Antonia Moropoulou, restoration scientific supervisor

The tomb of Jesus is in danger of collapse,
an engineering miracle required for safety
above the shrine's unstable foundations,
and just off the coast of Australia, four
of the stone-tower Apostles have drowned
in the sea where divers plunge to examine
the bodies of those who are underwater.
Cautionary scenarios, but from the shore,
near San Francisco, a local resident gladly
shows me where the famous earthquake's
epicenter lies offshore near Mussel Rock.

Where I live, thick stone supports are strung
across the Susquehanna River, remnants
of a bridge collapsed, decades ago, by torrents
of ice freed by heavy late-January rain.
A friend died in that flood, swept from his feet
and washed into catastrophe the night
before my school office took water as I typed
on a Saturday morning, a state policeman
knocking in a way that made me believe
my teenage son was dead until he asked
if I'd seen that friend reported missing,
saying nothing about the water that reflected
the bank of overhead fluorescent lights.
Nearly every summer, during dry spells,
a path of stones resurfaces in the river
near that friend's house, those rock laid down,
he once told me, by a cult leader who walked
on water, testing me, perhaps, for foolishness

years before he became the homeowner
who overstayed the rising water by an hour,
suffered, and was half-buried by a neighbor's
pickup truck. Upstream, an inflatable dam
is erected across the river each summer
for boating and fishing and floating parties
on a temporary lake where possibly
patterned rocks are buried so deeply
they are legends until October, stones
our locals attribute to the Oneida fording
from side to side in another century,
guides pointing to the cliff side above
a renovated bridge, the rock weathered
into what passes for the stark profile
of Chief Shikellamy, whose likeness
has watched his people and culture smothered
by coal and railroads until they were,
in turn, assigned to unemployment,
his name sewn, for nearly fifty years,
on the jackets worn by high school athletes.
No report I find speaks to his cliff's condition,
whether his face is in danger of crumbling,
whether imagination will be required
in order for anyone to believe an accident
of geology signifies even a small, local history.

Years ago, I watched a boy hurled from his bike
when it slipped into a rut formed overnight
by three hours of thunderstorms, his bare chest
and arms opened as if he'd been tortured.
That boy healed, but for days I walked
to that spot on the shoulder of our street
to evaluate the growth of that gully
until I believed it might surprise a car.
One morning, a township crew arrived
to chip-seal our street, pouring a thin coat
of hot asphalt to reinforce with truckloads
of scattered, jagged gravel. They placed

a series of orange cones to mark, I thought,
that rut for repair, promising safety until,
weeks later, they were removed, the gully
filled in with unearthed rocks a neighbor brought,
by wheelbarrow, from a construction site.

What's sensed is seldom balance. To pilgrims,
the temple constructed at the site of Christ's tomb
must have made heaven seem near, yet
it's been destroyed and restored three times.
Mussel Rock, John McPhee has written,
"is like a three-story building, standing
in the Pacific, with brown pelicans
on the roof where the San Andreas Fault
intersects the sea." Paragliders, now, are
frequent here, luminous in shafts of sun.
The remaining Apostles, made of limestone,
will be extinguished by the sea that will
create more, in time, from the current cliffs.
When a house was being built at the end
of our street, I spent an early evening
carrying the most decorative stones by hand
from where they had been turned up to where
I marked the edge of a hillside of flowers
and shrubbery and one cactus that shortly
overran that shallow wall to spread into the lawn,
and each summer, in a small ritual of saving,
I have inched those stones outward because
I will not mow those spine-filled leaves.

Limits

the Joshua trees
are vanishing
in an orderly way,
the last to die
those that flourished
at elevation
because it's become
too torrid for them
where tourists are
often forbidden
after ten a.m.,
the time when my wife
and I hiked, once,
in mid-August, at
one hundred and ten
degrees, both of us
stunned by what some
living things can stand
from a morning sky,
yet even such
adaptive trees have
limits this earth has
nearly reached, the park
posted, each day, like
a condemned building,
for latecomers who are
always willing to enter,
touring the terminal,
hushed by regret like
the newly penitent
while *inevitable* drives by
in his ancient, rusted car.

Fly Fishing, Parsing, the Faculty Retreat

After our visiting scholar presented
as overtly gay. After she focused
solely upon the explicitly sexual.
After our wealthy alumna donor
withdrew her support, in particular,
from the annual scholar's series,
the department, in response, held
an "identity retreat" seventy miles
from campus, the setting replete with
well-tended nature and amenities.
We circled our soft chairs to form
the language of our public statement,
deciding, in 1988, whether, in writing,
to move from *tolerate* to *celebrate*
in our official stance on differences.
One of us, after lunch, taught the nuances
of fly fishing in the site's promoted creek.
He displayed lures that varied by size
and color, a miscellany of wings
translucent or feathered, casting one
upon the water lightly as deception
while sunlight performed its shimmer.
Later, there was the American canon
to strip and reassemble, a roster
everyone could embrace. Diversity,
the chair reminded, was as limitless
as the insects. There were exercises
and prompts, model syllabi to share.
A woman said she loved hearing Spanish
in her grocery store. "One of my best friends"
was left unspoken. The staff served chicken,
fish, or plates of savory vegetables.
By the following morning, our statement
was reshaped, exactitude approved,

clauses refined, phrases repositioned.
To counter objection, three sentences were
parsed and diagrammed, a scan of isms
reweighed to confirm the heft of fairness.
At last, after congratulations were shared,
the passive voice packed and loaded
into nine separate cars that fostered
everyone's personal preference, I watched,
while the lot emptied, the fly fisherman cast
his line cleanly enough to muffle misery.
A few miles, it took, to shut off my radio,
a few more to park beside a meadow
so natural I walked knee-deep through
what I had no names for, listening,
for once, to languages other than my own,
wind, leaves, a myriad of insects,
the honest speech of scurry underfoot.

In the Era of Collective Thought

From a hospital in Texas,
one hundred brains have vanished
and, as always, we hurry to
use the colorful emoji
for smile and laughter when flurries
of posts suggest identity,
from genius to sociopath,
for whoever is responsible.
And yes, when we're alone, we ask
ourselves "For what?" and unable
to answer, we substitute "How?"
and evaluate the likelihood
of one brain at a time or one hundred
in a single, well-planned heist.
Weeks now, unaccounted for, the brain
of Texas sniper Charles Whitman,
the brains of the frequently concussed,
those in early dementia, those
whose last demand was suicide.
Tonight, after we lock our doors,
the alarm coded for our speech,
we speculate the thief lives
surrounded by so many brains
he cannot admit a guest.
That he must master home repair
or live among leaks and drafts
and dangerous wiring. All day,
the way it has been for weeks,
we have seen nobody outside.
As if our isolation has been
perfected by the relentless work
of the brain-eating zombies
we are fond of discussing like
curators of horror's garish gallery,

or as if we envy that thief
his museum of damaged brains.
Cerebrum, cerebellum--
we recite our parts like beginners
in anatomy, counting down to
the constancy of medulla
while the underworld's weather
loots the grid we rely upon.
Drought has master-minded
the overthrow of farming.
Rain is a hostage whose ransom
has been raised so high the sky
is unable to pay. Shut-ins,
we carry the memory of comfort
like a congenital hump.
Decisions made elsewhere are
hurtling toward us in rented trucks,
all of them explaining themselves
in a gibberish of slogans.

Pentecostal

Like carefully selected wine,
preparation is often paired
with prudence, the vigilance

of a single mother's Shepherd
reinforced by motion sensor.
Coyotes, some nights, rouse the dog

to barking before frightening
my daughter's floodlight to brilliance
when it confirms their trespass,

but that evening, carrying an axe,
a neighbor climbed her stairs
to declare he would kill her dog

and anyone who tried to stop him.
The steep, empty lot next door had
been cleared of brush and damage

to lessen the chance of wildfire.
As if emptied, every nearby house
was darkened, the street fleeing

like refugees, following safety
to see where it was going.
He crouched, a gargoyle

for the unbearable, four steps
between him and the entrance
to the radius of the axe handle

he hefted slowly from left to right.
For a moment, mystery would not

shut up. Motive lived at the far edge

of language. From somewhere close,
a car alarm began to moan inside
a garage like a weakening pulse.

From house to house, barking began, each
flaring light translating those speeches,
not into salvation, but reprieve.

Sparklers

1

Once, at the museum's retrospective
for Kirlian photography, a display
of fingertips fringed by fire, captions
that claim light swells and shrinks
to expose our psychic auras.
Next, a torso surrounded by light
perhaps exuded by the holy spirit,
that body's corona proof we are
as chosen as the arrangements
of constellations, disregarding
that those suns cluster, we know,
by the accident of distance and size.

2

Decades ago, I wrote my name
on air with sparkler flares, circled
brief, eclipsed suns or threw
their violent lace into an arc
that spiraled sparks to our lawn
where, July 5th, I had to find
every hurled wire from the night before.
Up and back, I paced our yard along
the narrow paths the mower took.
I failed, each year, to relight even
one wire, and some mornings, now,
I discover myself so thin and dark,
I fear I cannot be relit, even
by the acolyte of aging
in his white smock with scarlet hem.

3

One night, after baseball and the blasts

of complimentary fireworks
that opened nearly overhead,
the pedestrian bridge to Pittsburgh,
temporarily closed, compresses
our crowd of late-night walkers.
Someone next to my family
mentions the latest terror,
children and their mothers pierced
by an explosion of glittering spikes.
Faces of young girls illuminate
two nearby phones. Ahead of us
a father believes his arms
have invented safety.
The river's cruise ship passes
beneath us, its decks packed
with prom goers. The river reflects
a swirl of pinwheels; a vendor
ignites a fistful of sparklers.
Somewhere, terror dreams
our bodies as it decides
the exact address for delight.

4

Just now, I have learned that
some caves in New Zealand have
planetarium ceilings, their stars
systematized by the fixed, feeding
positions of glowworms, each
of those brilliant larvae claiming
a uniform space, spinning curtains
of threads to fish for food. Always,
in that ordered heaven, those worms
shine, their beacons drawing insects.
And sometimes, those larvae, transformed
at last, to clouds of gnats, are trapped
among the sticky filaments spun
by their children to be held and eaten.

After the Election News, Human Subjects

This morning, after the election news,
Human subjects were solicited with
Promises of fair pay, free room and board
Pending a required, on-site physical,
Sufficient prompt to send me to research.

Near Miami, I learned, are colonies
Of human subjects, people who take drugs
Without reading one line of disclaimer.
In Indianapolis, the homeless
And the drunk are recidivist subjects.

Overnight, swastikas had blossomed like
Post-rain, desert flowers. *Fucking Jew* had
Been photographed on local headstones.
In workshop, the four Jewish students sat
Side by side—"Solidarity," one said,
And the class laughed like they'd always realized
The country was a room reserved in hell.

An hour later, at the flea market
In a long-closed drive-in where speaker poles
Were the stripped teeth of huge, forgotten gears.
Water-damaged Bibles were being sold,
Forty percent off list. One Old Testament
Was stained through Esther; another
Was sound after the prophecies of Ezekiel.

Because speakers have value, the vendor
Explained. Because they're stolen for wiring
To televisions, and yes, he confessed,
Original list prices were unknown.
I started to think about promises

Sputtering like the generator that
Fueled his flimsy heat, how unimportance
Can lead some to ingest untested drugs,
The world's laboratory using our hearts
Again and again to see which of them
Turn anxious, or worse, to indifference.

What I wanted was erasure, an end
To pleasantries. At last, empty-handed,
I sped to the advertised location
For temporary work, a closed motel
Whose lot was near capacity with cars.
No vacancy, erased, was etched on air,
And I examined the makes and models
For disappointments that drove their owners
To waive their rights for risk's small salary.
I walked among those cars as if I had
A reason besides being a voyeur
For loss, risking only the side effects
Of the inexpressible empathy
That crowded into my car, chattering
Like a strange, unintended passenger.

2

CONTAGIOUS   (A Sequence)

Dance Mania

Within an early chapter
In the thick biography
Of hysteria, Frau Troffea
Suddenly lifts her arms
As if she's hanging laundry,
A spread-wide sheet. Hallelujah,
Perhaps, but then her feet
Skid into the swerve of dance,
Limbs chattering out of sync
With any tune her neighbors know.
There, in the sixteenth century,
Spectators gather like guests
For the first dance at weddings,
But she carries on for days, tranced
By some phantom partner
Who leads until someone joins,
Then another, so many more
In this weeks-long fit of dancing,
That ballroom fills four hundred strong,
Twisting to the inaudible,
The song on repeat, the pit keyed
To a frenzy of thrashing,
Each dancer with room enough
For solitary violence.
Nothing can end this except
Exhaustion or, for many, death,
The manic choreography
Famous for casualties
Who endured to the heart's collapse.

Miss Hartung Explains **Contagious**

Twice a week, during public health,
Miss Hartung filled the room with fear
While we sat in perfect rows marked
By small spots in the wax, the ones
That revealed restlessness, that shamed
If they showed like lace-edged slip hems.

The contagious, she said, leave filth
That lives on buses and streetcars
And seats at the Etna Theater.
What's worse, you'll never know who's been there
And given you the itch and fester.

The contagious, she said, shout words
You mustn't say. They seed their yards
With bottles, cans, and tires; drip snot
And never cover when they sneeze.
They wipe their noses on their sleeves
Where crusts collect like scabs that bleed.

The contagious borrow combs, touch fountains
With their mouths. They gobble food they've dropped
To floors. Not setting rings of paper,
They squat on public toilets, never scrub
With water that's been run to scalding hot.

The contagious are everywhere,
Common as flies. Splattering stains,
The contagious spread like lies.
Look around, you'll see what I mean.
Eyes open, class. Keep yourselves clean.

Children's Television

> *In Portugal, a children's soap opera produced mass hysteria, symptoms of the script's mysterious disease showing up in young viewers.*

Epidemic waits like the rocks
Below the cliff-carved narrow road.
It hums the synonyms
For inevitable, arranges them
In sentences slick with speed.

The script opens its sack of symptoms
To teach the country's children,
Each episode completed
Like homework. One mother fears
Permanent pockmarks; one follows
Her son's geometrical proof
Of cough and rash and fever,
Afraid of its solution.

All of them watch until the script
Declares an end to epidemic.
But after every child recovers,
After school reopens, parents
Learn that a child, next season,
Is crushed inside accident's car,
And all of them refuse to drive.

The Devil's Children

"The sins of your fathers," Miss Shaffer said,
"belong to you," and she listed the ways from drunk
to unfaithful while our Sunday school class
constructed heaven and hell, silently
attaching the future for all of us
onto the church's new bulletin boards.
Melanie Truman, whose father was gone,
cut narrow spaces into heaven's gate,

forming a grate so we could see inside
where white wings we drew floated against
a cloudless blue sky. We shaped a purple robe
for God and a loose, white cloak for Jesus,
their faces turned away because we dared
not look upon them. "The whirling of those white wings,"
Miss Shaffer said, "looks like it was created
by the sweet, benevolent breath of God."
All of us designed the black wings for hell.
Dick Wertz, his father arrested, scissored scarlet
triangles for eternal flames and left the green door
to hell wide open for the paired hands we made
by tracing ours. We forecast weather for hell,
heavy rain, every drop vanishing above the flames
because not one would ever reach us when
God saw into our sinful hearts that year
before boys and girls were separated
for Sunday School, before we began to learn
the sheer sins of lust and envy, using the sin
of falsehood to deny how we abused ourselves
and blasphemed, counting the commandments
we broke each day although Miss Shaffer made us sit,
one by one, beside the dark, detailed face
of Satan she drew, learning, each Sunday,
how it felt to be the devil's children.

The Bug-bite Commonality

> *In 1962, dressmakers in a textile factory blamed the bite*
> *of an unseen bug for the illness that spread among them.*

The dressmakers grew faint,
Unionized by the venom
Of a bug so elusive
The foreman had to search
Like a safety inspector.

Claims fluttered their small,

White wings until, at last,
Owners started the strip search
For evidence, bodies bared
For a physician's house call.

What, among insects, left
No mark as it poisoned?
Ask us, the dressmakers said.
Go ahead, and they answered
As if they'd taken vows

During suicide videos,
Each of them displaying
Scissors and needles,
Wearing a white mask
Over the nose and mouth.

When one of us dies, examine
Your flawless flesh. After the next,
Open her sewing machine
Like a music box, and its song
Will emerge like a spider.

My Mother Lists the Things that are Catching

Measles. Mumps. Chicken pox.
The flu. The common cold. Strep throat.
Whooping cough. Smallpox. Tuberculosis.
Head lice. Ringworm. Impetigo.
Poison ivy. Poison sumac. Poison oak.
Comic books. Television. Rock and roll.
Lying. Stealing. Cursing. Idle hands.

The Crusades

One Sunday, just before we were moved to the next "higher" class, Mrs. Shaffer said the Crusades were the pinnacle of holiness. "Imagine," she said, "a host of armies fighting for Christ." She told us about Peter the Hermit, the hero who preached so well Christians everywhere joined up to rescue the Holy Land from the heathens. "Because the struggle never ends," she said, "so many Christians wanted to march to Jerusalem, there was always a next Crusade. In 1213, there were 30,000 children who marched. Imagine that, boys and girls. Imagine them being willing to be martyrs for Christ."

The Trespasser Chronic

Because my sister had walked home
alone eight Fridays that summer,
this time carrying the green skirt
she'd sewn at 4-H, mastering
a straight, invisible seam,
she took a short cut through the yards
of tiny, flood plain houses
bunched like a small, silent herd.
She was eager, in August,
to enter that skirt and a dress
in the county fair, girls' novice class,
hundreds of preteen outfits
laid out for three shades of ribbons
two weeks after she identified
which loose dog, possibly rabid,
had bitten her as she crossed
that neighborhood of the unleashed,
so hesitant, when she'd narrowed
the choice to two, that both were loaded
into a van while the owners cursed,
the rest of that pack of dogs
barking as if they were
marking her, as if, next time,
they'd make sure she'd never tell.

Tulipmania

In the early seventeenth century,
in the Netherlands, tulips from Turkey
charmed everyone. They loved Holland's soil.
New breeds were coveted. The price of bulbs
went up. There were mornings when so many
people woke to what seemed like paradise,
the rich had to own the best of those bulbs.
Speculators in bulbs made huge profits,
and buyers, eager to be rich, bought bulbs
on credit. At last, the price of a bulb
rose to as much as the equivalent
of two million dollars. When the bubble
burst, the deepest believers were ruined.

Ugsomeness

> *n. (archaic) loathsome*

On television, politicians
Lift from disaster's leaves like starlings,
Their thick-flocked chatter sending shudders
Through the room of held drinks and hors d'oeuvres.

Somebody suggests, "Fear and loathing,"
Producing applause as if a book
Will follow that allusive title.
Ugsomeness, I tell them, the tough,

Archaic word better suited
To measure the circumference of rage,
And not willing to explain, I walk
Out the door and stare at the still life

Of the neighbor's house, time slowing down
Like accident's traffic, this loathing
Setting flares before it lifts its paws.
After a while the inside voices

Begin to smear like an overstrike.
Loud talk infects the living room, turning
From politics to the poor and dark who,
Quite frankly, they're tired of hearing about,

Someone shouting "ugsome!" and receiving
A spontaneous round of laughter.
For now, alone, there's a sensation
Of stillness that I understand is

The hell side of immortality,
This loathing so lame in familiar
English, yet extending as far as
The infinite integers for pi.

The Space-Junk Premonition

One autumn, my son searched the sky
For the first sign of space junk tumbling
Precisely toward us, sleeping downstairs
And walking eyes-up, expectant.

He researched each satellite,
Its size and orbit. He prophesized
At school, at last infecting
Boys and girls with binoculars

Who, for hours, scanned overhead,
A pinpoint of hysteria
In Selinsgrove, Pennsylvania
Where they anticipated craters

As if they were following
Invasion bulletins. Each of them
Slept in their basements, and each woke
Believing a terror of fragments
Had torn apart someone they loved,
A skeptic in an upstairs room.

A Citizenry of Birds

Tarantulas leave behind footprints of silk—Harper's

A neighbor, shortly after sunrise,
Says he loves to hear English
In the morning from his backyard birds.

They're citizens, he tells me, born here,
So many generations
With us, their accents have disappeared.

His mouth flexes. The pink horizon
Has nearly vanished. We are
Surrounded by the bright eggs of May.

My nod, meant to be neutral, narrows
The distance to empathy.
Only our lawns show the paths of shoes.

Suddenly, along our street, houses
Are raising flags, becoming
The embassies of allied countries.

When a siren opens full-throated
On the nearby county road,
I try to translate its accident.

Squalled from his architecture of leaves,
Vowels seem a needle's cry
Seeking a sample of suspect blood.

Some of the letters cannot be sung;
His lawn displays the sparkling,
Bent admission to his blue-rimmed door.

A Month of Crusaders

March 29th   Moscow, two women detonate on the Metro, 40 dead

March 31st   Kislyar, two bombers, 12 dead

March 31st   Khyber, Pakistan, one car bomber, 6 dead

April 4th   Baghdad, three car bombers, 42 dead

April 9th   Ingushetia, Russia, one woman detonates, 2 dead

April 12th   Mosul, Iraq, one car bomber, 3 dead

April 19th   Peshawar, Pakistan, one bomber, 26 dead

April 23rd   Baghdad one car bomber, 11 dead

April 26th   Sana'a, Yemen, one bomber, 1 dead

April 28th   Baghdad, two car bombers, 5 dead

Possession

In the 17th century, in Loudun, Mother Superior Jeanne des Agnes claimed the spirit of Urbain Grandier, the parish priest, visited her at night to seduce her. Soon other nuns reported spectral foreplay, moaning in ecstasy at night, convulsing and speaking in tongues during the day. Exorcism followed, but the nuns remained possessed by the demons Asmodeus and Zabulon who had entered the convent with a bouquet of roses thrown over the wall by Grandier.

When possession went public, crowds of thousands come to watch Out of the nuns' mouths flowed public blasphemy. From the files of the exorcist came the contract from Asmodeus himself, signed in blood by Grandier, a host of demons, and Satan himself. That contract has been saved for centuries, so that long after Grandier was burned at the stake, those nuns recanting and regaining their holiness, we can witness Satan's pitchforked signature and the decorative names of the demons.

The Martyr in our Town

The martyr in our town is scouting
The public places where we gather
In great numbers. He enters our malls
And notes the busiest stores; he scans
The food court's longest lines. Fridays,
He watches football at the high school;
Saturdays, a blockbuster film.
Sundays, there are churches to attend,
Sitting with families on wooden pews.

The martyr in our town studies
Prophecies and commandments. He reads
Only the holy translations. At last,
When winter justifies his knee-length coat,
He thickens his waist with dynamite,
Develops a nails and ball-bearings paunch.
He enters the one restaurant where
Every diner has three forks, two spoons,
And wine on ice, ticking as he gives
His reservation name. He decides
That the tables nearby are perfect
With use, steps forward as the hostess
Offers a complimentary room
For his heavy coat. All this, he prays,
Will spread, go airborne, a pandemic
Contagion. She employs the word "sir"
Just as he triggers himself, ascending.

THE MUSSOLINI DIARIES

1

A mother and daughter produce thirty volumes of Benito Mussolini's diaries. The older woman perfects Mussolini's handwriting well enough to fool Mussolini's son and a university expert, who exclaims, "Thirty volumes of manuscript cannot be the work of a forger, but of a genius." *The Sunday Times of London*, eleven years after the forgery is exposed, buys, from those same women, $71,400 worth of pages to publish.

2

Starting with ovals, Miss Hartung said, it was time for third grade to master cursive and the use of the fountain pen. "Around, around, around," she chanted. "Dip, swirl, and don't rest the tip on the paper." We earned As and inkwells. We had blotters from the bank, last month stamped on each one. March was a comic wind and a valiant vault while we wrote a letter to our parents, signing our names, and I added my perfect signature to where it said BOOK OWNER on the inside covers of every copy of a history book on the shelves in the back of the room, repeating it like a serial I expected to become a novel.

3

In seventeenth century England, a religious allegory was published. Entitled *A Wordless Book*, it totaled eight blank pages: two black for evil, two red for redemption, two white for purity, two gold for eternal bliss.

In 1738, Hermann Boerhaave died and left one copy of a self-published, sealed book, *The Onliest and Deepest Secrets of the Medical Art*. The book sold for $20,000 at auction and, when the new owner opened it, everything but the title page was blank.

Thomas Wirgman arranged his self-published books by page color. He spent $200,000 to produce his work, trying to get the sequence of colors exactly right. Purple, orange, blue, yellow, brown--a possibly sublime first chapter, a pattern to engage all readers. Yellow, green, red, green, yellow, blue. Altogether, he sold six copies, misunderstood like a genius.

The salesman who wants me to buy a blank book, each of its leather-bound pages white, says they mitigate grief. "Turn the pages slowly," he says. "Linger a bit on each one. You'll see."

4

A student is ecstatic about her first publication. She has been sending out letters to editors for several years, reading magazines at random and submitting hundreds of letters on whatever subject moved her to write, perfecting the epistolary mode.

5

Once, Gandhi wrote a letter to Charles Atlas, asking, "I wonder if there is some way you can build me up?" He wanted to try Dynamic Tension, the science of pitting one muscle against another. And because Atlas, as he claims, felt sorry "for the poor chap, nothing but a bag of bones," he sent Gandhi his instructions for free.

6

During the reign of Ming emperor Yung Lo (1403-1425), an 11,095 volume encyclopedia was compiled and written. Because of its length, it was too expensive to be published.

Hendrik Hertzberg produced a book called *One Million*. In varying numbers, each chapter consisted entirely of dots.

The 1886 *Appleton's Cyclopedia of American Biography* contained 84 phony biographies submitted by an unknown correspondent. For years, some of those entries stayed. It took until 1936 to weed out the final fraud.

7

One summer I stole the letter to my parents that listed my grades. I changed the F I'd received to a B and retallied my quality points, my credits, and my grade point average. I added up fictitious sums in columns crowded close to the typed numbers I'd altered. As if I were figuring alternate grade points. As if I were anticipating one of my final grades being changed by a sympathetic professor. Something to account for all those diversions, each a reason not to look closely at the lie I'd created because it was temporary and certain to be improved.

8

I smiled when I read about the Septuagint, how there were 72 translators, six from each of the 12 tribes of Israel who worked in separate rooms, and when they finished and compared, all of their work was identical. But then all six newspapers in the library began with the same sentence because a celebrity was accused of murder.

9

The valentine of coincidence is bordered by old doilies: Some numerologists claim Shakespeare helped write the Bible. The evidence: The King James Version was published in 1610 when Shakespeare was 46 years old; *Shake* is the 46th word of Psalm 46; *Spear* is the 46th word from the end of Psalm 46.

10

When I was a boy, our house held seven Bibles--King James, the Revised, one with a thick concordance. They lay open to highlighted verses or stood closed beside photographs of owners long dead. Every word in each was true and perfect and surged through the filaments of my body until I glowed with hope. I breathed the dust of generations gone to glory. I memorized, word for word, scriptures selected for the growing boy.

11

Vortigern and Rowena is the play William Henry Ireland claimed was written by Shakespeare. Ireland forged love letters from Shakespeare to Anne Hathaway; he wrote the cursive script for a drawer full of personal papers, convincing James Boswell of their authenticity. That play was performed at the Drury Lane Theater in 1796, jeered by the audience, who knew Shakespeare, apparently, better than handwriting analysts did.

12

For years a man named William Key claimed the word SEX is visible in Lincoln's beard on every five-dollar bill. For America's confidence, Key explained. It's there as a subliminal surge reminding us to save or spend, with ease, our currency. He published directions to its sighting, and I've followed his map to ink blots which, on every one of the fifty five-dollar bills I've tested, spells nothing.

13

"The history of passion will tumble this week," I read, Pennsylvania slicing off a crumbling cliff where rockslides threaten one of its highways. The newspaper suggests a reunion, asking former defacers to gather for an hour, and I park off Route 28, north of Pittsburgh, to read the graffiti of desire. There are dozens of cars, fifty of us looking up at the hand-over-hand history of lust, and I pick out Doreen and Clarice, Monica and Donna, reading nearby faces like name tags at a conference, deciding whether or not they're still paired with Chuck and Ron, Woody and Buck. I think Gary + Sharon, still visible, is a forgery because

I can't remember the boy who risked himself seventy feet above this traffic, that nobody else at the base of this blackboard would have struggled into danger and printed anything but his nickname before he added the full spelling of the girl he'd love forever.

14

Alcibiades Simonides, during the 19th Century, forged a manuscript of Homer, sold it to the king of Greece, who first consulted scholars at the University of Athens, each of them saying "Yes" to authenticity.

15

A mile from Gary + Sharon, a Dairy Queen has become The Lighthouse Bible Baptist Church. The signboard's letters spell times and themes and ALL WELCOME under the multiple ramps of a bypass. The church bulletin replaces the menu as if you could bend to the sliding glass window to order salvation.

16

In the Greenwood Cemetery, two miles above the Dairy Queen church, lies a swath of relatives. Four of these gravesites are flowering, four are not. The geraniums bloom red for my grandmother, two great uncles and one aunt; the other four relatives lie bare. My sister, when I tell her, says, "That's the way I always do it." As if she were singing a chorus after verses I'm supposed to know for the ballad of the favored.

17

A student says he's transcribed thousands of words from H. P. Lovecraft because that language makes him the world's greatest writer. "Necrosis," he reads from his notebook. "Mephitic. Nobody else could ever think of those." I offer "emesis" and "lavage," two ways to rid characters of the possession of poisons. He writes both words as if a story were beginning.

18

Ern Malley, in 1944, was published in *Angry Penguins*, a magazine that proclaimed him as one of two giants of Australian poetry. He had just died at 25, the large selection of his poems submitted by his grieving sister. Each one of those poems had been copied, bits and pieces of various books pasted together by two bored soldiers.

19

When Nancy Luce wrote poems, she inscribed them on the eggs she gathered, adding the name, when she finished, of the chicken who'd laid that tablet. Like a dedication, since all of her poems were about those chickens she raised and loved, psalms in their praise.

20

Verses have been embossed on pins, carved into the walls of caverns and tombs. Poems have been traced in water, fire, and air. My father refused his meals without the brief poem of prayer. He gripped my visitor's hand and recited the rhymed passages of praise and thanks as if I'd gobble that food while he recited over the bacon and eggs that welcomed morning.

21

When a criminal named George Cudmore was executed in 1830, his skin was used to bind a book, Milton's *The Poetical Works*, someone's notion of the odd possession.

22

Clifford Irving, in 1971, deceived five handwriting experts hired by his book publisher. All of them agreed it was the genuine Howard Hughes who wrote the supporting documents to verify the authenticity of the interviews for the forthcoming biography. For Irving to forge such an amount of material "would be beyond human ability," said one expert.

23

The photographic memory champion lives in Burma, reciting, so far, seventeen thousand pages of Buddhist books. He's memorized all of those volumes; someone else is compelled to read along for verification.

24

On the last afternoon of her life my mother wrote and mailed her weekly news to me. After the funeral, after I traveled home, I received her note from the neighbor who'd held my mail. That letter lay warm in my hands; it yellowed and curled from the air I was drawing toward me and the language on the page. The signature in flames, I saw the return address affixed in the envelope's corner as it's supposed to be, insurance against loss.

3

The Election Remembers the Challenger Disaster

Satellites were boring, those metal balls
splashing into the ocean,
parachutes trailing like skirts.

Nobody needed the moon anymore,
nothing but rocks and powder,
a place we'd never visit.

But we loved the Shuttle like a hit song—
women in space, congressmen,
a teacher so familiar

we anticipated bankers on board,
salesmen in helmets, each job
a ticket to split the sky.

Who tried to delay that launch? Some doubter,
the sort of guy who'd never
apply and train for orbit.

Those engineers. They're the ones ridiculed
in high school. Why listen now
to the old whine of caution?

The memos were shredded like old money.
Tensile strength. Heat resistance.
Fear of unusual cold.

Look, when we saw the woman who would teach
our children, we remembered
the answers to test questions

we'd left blank, finished the long-due essays.

The O-ring was an item
we purchased in quantity

at the hardware store. Like screws. Like washers.
Things tossed into kitchen drawers
with the stuff we sometimes need.

All this morning, and then all afternoon,
questions resurrected like
film clips, the answers practiced:

Indelible? Unforgivable? Well loathed?
Not to our knowledge. Most unlikely. No.

The Substitute Teacher Explains Climate

Listen closely, children, winter is
an aging relative who will visit
infrequently at first, then not at all.
Be happy to wear your clumsy boots
and mittens. Already, your snowmen
are crawling north like bark beetles,
those refugees who will slaughter
your forests like a swarm of saws.

Because, thousands of miles from here,
the ice is thinning, floods will fill your lives.
Even at the North Pole, a meltwater lake
has formed. In Greenland, in one day,
twelve billion tons of ice have melted.
All of you know the power of taboo.
Whisper "climate change" to each other
like a favorite, filthy forbidden word.
Soon enough, you will say it aloud.
Trust me, it's as imminent as sex.
Those men who will not repeat it
have chosen to save only themselves.

Remember how the wildfire last time
leveled Paradise to a stencil for hell?
This year, fires are ravaging the Arctic.
The wind, children, loves embers so much
it sometimes carries them safely for miles.
Always check to see what's tumbling
and floating with the seeds and spores.
Those pretty things will descend by chance
to where destruction can root and prosper.

The Magician's Son

> *If a living being breathes ether, the body becomes as light as a balloon.*
> —Robert-Houdin, magician

In the first anesthesia years,
I was inflated by medicine's
Magic. Nightly, I returned
To the near-death of ether.
My father taught me to dress
Properly to float, but the truth
Is the buoyancy smell always
Spread from behind the curtain
Rather than the bottle passed
Empty beneath my nose.
My father said the audience
Was suspended as well,
Between wonder and disgust,
That all of those fathers,
Considering their limits
Of sacrifice, were relieved when
I awoke, blinking as I dropped
Back into the familiar world.
Always, however, I walked stiffly,
My trickery suit so awkward
I looked to be lamed by gas.
Those fathers must have imagined
Putting their sons at such risk,
Miracles who could suddenly die.
There was a collective holding
Of breath, fear wafting over them.
Though it might kill him, what father
Doesn't want his son to fly?
But listen, after the ether era,
My father never again showed

Such care and tenderness.
Height became ordinary without
The framework for flying.
My upstairs window was a mouth
Through which I thrust my head.
And yes, I loved looking
Straight down, leaning at the waist.
The trembling. The anticipation
Of screaming. My body balanced
By the memory of an odor.

Carp are Dying of Herpes in Babylon

After Harper's, *April 2019*

In Wyoming, a house cat
has been diagnosed with plague.
In India, an elephant calf
has died from anthrax, which,
in Malawi, has claimed
the lives of forty-five hippos.

Outbreaks of salmonella,
less deadly, but more common,
have been triggered world-wide
by chicken nuggets in Canada,
powdered milk in France,
a pet hedgehog here at home.

Always, it's the exotic that
fascinates—Rift Valley Fever,
Seneca Valley Virus, the names
reassuringly localized, as foreign
as Ebola, now found airborne
by a particular Liberian bat.

For the familiar swine fever,
measures, of course, are taken,
the slaughtering, by the thousands,
of Japanese hogs, Denmark fencing
its border to protect itself from
the threat of infected boars.

Those responses, naturally,
have been applauded. Something
must be sacrificed or barred

for the country's greater good,
and so far, after all, it's merely
been animals, the decisions

difficult only in the abstract.
Although yes, it's been verified
that people remember better
what is said if the memory
of a sentence remains,
until its very end, unclear.

The Anxiety of Dams

> *"Hope is part of the strategy there"*
> —Lake Oroville Dam report

Difficult, the daily variations
Of violence, discovering its names
In the small sorrows of diminishment
And the perjuries of a president.

In the present in which we are bitter,
We follow the plight of dams exhausted
By an astonishment of rain, breaching
Become a citizen of possible.

Elsewhere, in the desert where betrayal
Is finishing its memoir, the nameless
Who are sorting the ordinary hear
Nothing about the ache of old mistakes.

As in the warning sermons, Mosul Dam
Is built on earth that cannot sustain it.
Not sand exactly, but rock so porous
It needs, perpetually, to be filled.

An exercise in eternity, that
Stuffing, someone minding the task in shifts,
Yet this dam is sinking inch by fraction
Of an inch, sufficient, soon, to stress cracks

In the assurances of safety's face.
But listen, it's not only those thousands
Who are living in a death zone. Millions
Far downstream have been deceived by distance,

Their bodies scripted as the "swept away,"
Those, too, dead without names in the legends
Of the fall, listed by the neighborhoods
Of pride, indifference, and disbelief.

How to Survive the Pandemic: A Litany

Practice cough etiquette--
a tissue or your inner elbow,
never your palm.

This is the other side of stone

Avoid touching
your eyes, your mouth, your nose.

This is the other side of water

Begin social distancing,
closing schools and day cares.

This is the other side of walls

Elsewhere, avoid crowds.

This is the other side of screens

If that is impossible,
maintain distance from others.

This is the other side of names

Beware rumors and fake news.

This is the other side of eyes

When things worsen, isolate yourself
and your family inside your home,
practicing "shelter in place."

This is the other side of doors

Be sure to have cached
at least two weeks
of water, food, and medicine.

This is the other side of future

To minimize contact
with the sick in your home,
designate a room for quarantine.

This is the other side of comfort

Wear a filter mask if you need to.

This is the other side of flesh

Buy the masks ahead of time
because there will be a shortage.

This is the other side of story

A new vaccine will take months.

This is the other side of fear

Remember that those
at greatest risk will receive it first.

This is the other side of jealousy

Get to know your neighbors
because you will need their help.

This is the other side of intimacy

Don't let fear erode empathy.

This is the other side of prayer

In the last great pandemic,
the sick often starved to death
because those still healthy
were terrified to go near them.

This is the other side of beginning

Perspective

Yesterday, as if it had knocked,
one mantis on the screen door
at eye-level demanded
a few minutes of shielded,
private welcome for the pastime
of imagining invasion
scaled to ordinary size.

*The praying mantis has five eyes: three simple ones lined
along the middle of its forehead that probably see only light and dark,
and two compound eyes for seeing colors and images.*

Time, too, for remembering
the alternate perspective
of B-movies, extravagances
of size featured, once, in each
double feature where radiation
birthed enormous spiders
and ants, lizards, an octopus . . .

*Despite its five eyes, the praying mantis is thought
to have only one ear, located in a slit in the thorax,
which allows the insect to hear ultrasonic sounds.*

. . . though in *The Deadly Mantis*,
one Saturday, radiation
was never mentioned while
stock footage showed an iceberg
calving from a glacier
just before the giant mantis,
naturally grown, was freed.

*The praying mantis can rotate
its triangular heads in almost a full circle,*

a feature not shared by other insects.

When I watched that film, years later,
with my cousin, he laughed and talked
over the dialogue, his hands often
clutching the air in front of his face.
A child, he said, could create better effects
for "the most dangerous monster that
ever lived!" as it ravaged and devoured.

When the mantis draws its legs up and folds them
under its head, it resembles a human's praying posture.
In actuality, this is the mantis' hunting position.

Decades have passed. Whatever
magnifies my cousin's lifelong tics
has settled and gripped. Parkinson's,
perhaps, or some internal wiring
short-circuited to a set of symptoms
pronounced enough to avert my eyes
from his murder of tremors.

When the mantis sights its prey, it lashes out with its front legs
to capture, then uses the long spikes that line its upper legs
to secure, allowing the mantis to eat at its leisure.

This morning I watched the same
or another mantis grasp a hummingbird
at the backyard feeder. In actual size,
the mantis began to chew that bird's head,
appetite guiding it to the brain. Horrible,
and yet busy past my willingness
to let routine call me inside, but

I recalled that B-movie and the spasms,
last week, that prevented my cousin
from passing bread and salad,
the conversation about climate change

that quickly began, hurricanes
and wildfires obscuring the terror
that accompanied the knife and fork.

Soeur Sourire and the Vanishing of Nuns

1
After your student's accidental death,
You calligraphy her workshop poem
About the possibilities of love,
Reforming the imagery for desire
With intricate loops and decisive slants.
Her setting is the garden of St. Paul
Tended by two ancient nuns who, each day,
Inspect the light altered by arrangements
Of decorative trees; who prune, monthly,
The rose bushes to allow kneeling for
The raised right hand of a smiling Mary.
Pausing, you remember it has been years
Since you have noticed a nun. Because they
Have abandoned their habits, you decide,
And remember how they rode the streetcar
In pairs; how they gathered at the museum
Where you were transfixed by dinosaur bones,
Mummies, and animals stuffed and mounted.
The way, for decades, perfectly preserved,
Lenin's body has proved that death flatters
Just as well as a costly, tailored suit.

2
Years ago, you learned that when the Germans,
During World War II, neared St. Petersburg,
The Communists moved Lenin's body to
Siberia, where almost anything,
Prisoner to icon, could be hidden.
Lately, in Florence, surrounded by faith,
You were startled by loud, recorded "Shhhs,"
A single "Silencio" from above
Meant to minimize a thousand tourists.

Your camera was shuttered by decree;
Everyone listened through rented ear buds
To the near-whisper of the guide, and some
Paid for candles to light and wish upon.
You shuffled close to a sarcophagus
Roped off like a crime scene. This saint, the guide
Murmured, was so selfless her body was
Shared by the cathedrals in competing
Cities, and you wanted to interrupt
To explain how the soldiers who guarded
Lenin's body, longing for usefulness,
Drank themselves daily into sorrowful songs
While Lenin lay silent. How, recently,
In Covington, Kentucky, you walked through
The landscaped grounds of a Benedictine
Monastery where monks had constructed
Monte Casino, forming, from limestone,
The world's tiniest chapel--six by nine,
Cell-sized, maximum occupancy three,
A pew where you sat as if believing
You heard the sacred urge of "save yourself"
Tumbling from the belfry too small for bells.

3

Your student's sixteen lines were a gospel
Of surfaces, touch after touch where nerves
Nearly breach the skin. They detailed blossoms
That flourished like sacrifice; they added
Topiary that shadowed erosions
From frequent storms, the nuns often singing.
You recalled *Soeur Sourire*, the Singing Nun,
Her song about Dominique relentless
On the radio, her Ed Sullivan
Minutes, how you followed her brief career,
Discovering she had left the order
For a woman, nothing certain by then
But the pull of desire. Nuns in the mall
Laughed so loudly you dreamed them touching each

Other or men they once had disciplined
In schoolrooms, hissing the "Shhh" of holy
Admonishment while their habits rustled.

4
The priest who blessed your wedding fled the church
For a woman who had spent seven years
As a nun. Soon Sister Smile killed herself,
Nuns becoming improbable as faith.
Already, a collection of habits
Is on display at your city's museum
Where teachers gather their restless students
To hear a young, uniformed guide explain
What those dark, dowdy outfits signified.
Her skirt stops short enough to turn your head
Toward her mystery, and you meditate
On which vows she would be willing to break,
Her history yammering somewhere else.

5
Before you left that cathedral, eighteen
Of the thirty-nine in your tour group dipped
Their fingers into an ornate basin
And skittered their dripping hands through the sign
Of the cross, "Shhh, Silencio" pausing
The guide, who nodded, as reverent in
Ancient, natural light as your student,
Who, at last, shifted to the white statue
Of the garden saint, his blessed hand smooth
From centuries of kisses, her poem
Ending in an astonishment of prayer.

The Importance of Captions

In this World War II retrospective, large,
yet exclusively Nazi point-of-view,
we see their dead and wounded, their rubble
enhanced by crying children, but at last
we pause to contemplate, held by women
in uniform, laughing and beautiful
and likely, by their poses, a little drunk.
They look to be celebrating. One man,
his chest a veteran's share of medals,
has strapped on an accordion and seems
so comfortable we guess he's just played
something peppy to whistles and applause,
pleasure so unanimous we assume
the early years when victories occurred
so readily that music was common.
But no, the caption reveals *late summer,
1944*, so merriment might
have been brief, even if the news from France
had been cleansed effectively by censors.
By then, they might have been celebrating
their fortunate posting, combat elsewhere
than southern Poland. The women, we read,
had been sworn in as "maids" to serve the guards
and administrators, a benefit
welcomed by everyone according to
the cheerfulness of camaraderie,
their part of the war with little danger
or unpleasantness. Maintenance mostly,
the occasional culling of the crowd
of prisoners, a sacrifice they were
willing to make for the Fuhrer, a small,
but important thing, tending to Auschwitz,
their song reaching the nearest prisoners,

perhaps some traditional melody
that many would recognize, even in
a foreign language, the tune remaining
with them, a few even mouthing the words
transported by the single syllable
of wind that accompanied the chorus.

The Nocturnal Age

1

Through our town's two red lights, speeding,
a white jeep strikes a woman with whom
I worked. Pauses, then flees. Barely,
she survives. For months, wheelchaired.
For short distances, at last, a walker.

Pending test results, the driver of interest
a man who lives within a mile, who drinks
nightly in a bar where he's recognized,
yet served, buying drinks for women who
might climb into that not-yet-impounded car.

Sympathy lingers for weeks, sighs before
moving on. Soon, she loses the job that
made her colleague, the call arriving
from the company's main office more
than a thousand miles from here.

2

Along that same main street, a self-
declared church enters a vacant store.
On folding chairs, the congregation
sits as quietly as the truth, the street
becoming the spirit of look-both-ways,
a parable now, shriveling into
a small, unhappy replica of comfort.

A donor volunteers a scooter, one,
he explains, that had saved his life.
The gift-giver, in the newspaper's
large photo, appears bent and fragile.
In a jaunty font, *Pride Go-Go*

is splashed across the scooter's side.
The donor's hand rests on a handlebar
as if he relies upon it for balance.

3
Those test results, after months,
become promises. After a year,
they are lies. The anniversary
repeats her name in the paper on
an inside page where a scientist
claims contemporary life may be
withering the hippocampus.

During depression, he says,
it seems to shrink, so vulnerable
to daily stress that the names
for common things can vanish.
Memories are early departures,
the ability to make new ones
already on red-eyes to where
the mind will arrive unattended.

Sometimes, he says, there is solace:
the damaged hippocampus might
never again make new memories,
but older memories are often safe.
My colleague had been a dancer.
Two witnesses can still repeat
the exact details of hit-and-run.
The victim has lost her right kidney.
The police still insist upon patience.

4
Those test results, two years and
counting, are unreported, but just now
that woman has been discovered dead
in another country. Tonight, the wind
claws so quietly at the door,

I imagine regret has come begging.
When the light dims, lies that feed where
the lawn disappears at honeysuckle
creep closer, sniffing the air, satisfied
there is so little danger they can risk
exposure. They crawl under the deck
where *acquiesce* has built a burrow,
stuffing themselves on perennials
while whispering reassurances:
"And still." "And yet." "Despite that."
cadenced by the brain stem into
the weakening heartbeat of epitaph.

The killing street, at her witching hour,
appears to be something close to blank.
A lone, low-watt bulb illuminates
a makeshift pulpit in the otherwise
vacant store front near where her car
was parked. Someone could crawl
across the street and rise unharmed.
Such supposing is what substitutes
for insight. Above the vacant store,
the glow of past-midnight television
illustrates the book of sleeplessness.
A single car pauses at the stop light
as if the extended absence of traffic
is a local omen for entrapment.

The Drownings of W.C. Fields

One summer, the century soon ending,
Fields practices his juggling while he works
A concession at the beach where, three times
Each day, he wades into the Atlantic
Like a tourist and swims to his drowning.

> *Yesterday I spoke with a woman who,*
> *Seventeen years ago, lost a swimmer*
> *While lifeguarding. Hand-over-hand, a boy*
> *Had edged to deep water along the dock*
> *That claimed part of a lake for summer camp.*

Each time, suffering the fireman's carry,
Fields goes so limp he terrifies a crowd
That circles near the junk-food stand that pays
For perfect timing, how long to perform
The life-and-death before he gags and spits.

> *No matter the reason, he'd lost his grip*
> *And gone under while she'd scolded a boy*
> *For running, adding a minute between*
> *Her whistles for buddy checks. "Last warning,"*
> *She'd said. "Don't let me see that again."*

And the crowd? After Fields, still dripping, stands,
They are ravenous from proximity
To tragedy, his colleagues arriving
With popcorn and candy, working that throng
Before price becomes a thing to ponder.

> *Twice each night, she said, she rises to check*
> *The breathing of her children who sleep paired*
> *In two rooms. A trilling in her ears says*

> *Evaluate the pillows, examine*
> *The chests for the relief of rise and fall.*

Dressed again, Fields resumes his juggling
And thinks of gin. Sometimes, he overhears
A shared version of his recent drowning.
Not once, that summer, is he recognized.
Always, the lucky victim is a fool.

> *Often, she said, her dreams are whistles and*
> *Screams. Always, there is water-with-shadow,*
> *A still life framed by memory's limits.*
> *Waking has weight yoked by her arms, kisses*
> *Repeatedly offered, yet unreturned.*

Imagine yourself watching a boy dragged
From the ocean, his chest being compressed
To resurrect breath. How hungry you are
For story to spew at acquaintances.
Insist your appetite is shared, safety
Impossible, and there is never shame
In the inability to comfort.

How Silly Grew

From selig, meaning holy, then innocent, then gullible, then foolish

1
Consider World War II's Operation Fu-Go,
The Japanese floating pidgin obscenity
Over the ocean, bomb-filled balloons on missions
As ludicrous as carrier pigeons to the moon,
Yet one of them blown to Oregon and gone off,

Killing six picnickers who thought the war over
Or so far away in May, 1945,
They must have guessed "a pet lost by the idle rich"
Or "Macy's Parade blown west," some children's cartoon
Color-promoted on the side they could not see.

2
Listen closely to my grandmother recalling
The great foolishness of Radithor, men who drank
The radium potion and internally glowed
From the aphrodisiac of atomic weight
Until collapsed inside, microwaved by desire.

Or watch that grandmother, whose husband swore by beer,
Rush into our "blind men walking" when one of us
Extended his stiffened arms through glass, tearing through
An artery and pumping blood like a lesson
In the awful foolishness of caricature.

3
Observe how seriously we played our war games,
How I crouched among the cherry trees and squinted,
Knowing my throat would be slit by the rubber knives
Of the clear-sighted, those who believed maneuvers
Mattered, who slaughtered for Operation Orchard,

The same site where I slapped myself down for sled-rides
After dark, so nearsighted I turned miracle
Throughout three blind slides before I hammered one stump
Head-on, earning a two-foot shear of skin instead
Of paralysis. What's more, I rose like those men

In war films who murmur, "It's only a flesh wound,"
Amazed by the precise location of escape,
And I summoned my own misuse of what's holy:
Vows in the snow to be sinless, to not covet
One item on the long list we carry like genes,

Speaking the soft benediction of renewal,
Putting aside the brief numbness of the crash site,
The booted journey home, not yet knowing how frail
Our claims to anything, that we're measured by pain
Endured like some St. Appolonia, whose teeth

Were pulled for not renouncing an indifferent God,
Another operation in the gallery
Of the holy where every tested face turns flat
As the dogma of brotherhood, as belief in
Eternity extended by diet and drugs,

By exercise and machinery and transplant.
And given that, we fear all of ourselves gone numb
In an enormous anesthesia while we read
Our way back to the source of one word, say *selig*
As if it were the first reply from paradise.

The Museum of American Tragedy

Bonnie and Cyde's V-8, the national tour.
Buford Pusser's Corvette, the "Walking Tall"
Memorial in Pigeons Forge, Tennessee.

Cannibal Ed Gein's corpse-carrying Ford,
"The car that hauled the dead from their graves,"
On the summer circuit of county fairs.

And James Dean's silver Porsche, now dismantled,
Thousands of fans hauling scrap metal home
Until death cars went under glass like jewelry.

Like Jayne Mansfield's Buick, its roof peeled back,
So anyone can see, at the Museum
Of American Tragedy, how she died,

According to the pitted sign, holding
Her Chihuahua, which died too, in the fog.
And, no doubt, every town sports a homemade

Fatal Accident Museum, drivers who retrace
The local death highways with needles set
At published speeds, excited as the millions

Who drive Kennedy's parade route, glancing
Back and up, scanning the grassy knoll near
The Dallas Assassination Museum.

A mile from here, at Keller's Auto Body,
Sits our town's latest death car, twisted
And torn and dumped out front where traffic

Creeps with exclamations and cameras.

Some of us, though, travel elsewhere to enter
The huge models at the Hands-On Institute

Where we tour our extravagant bodies,
Walk the huge arteries like blood clots
Or aggressive cells, terrorized by

The amplified heart, lost in the lungs
As if we were climbing the mountainous
Rib cage, another hour's journey from here,

Of diplodocus or brontosaurus
At the Dinosaur Gardens Prehistorical Zoo,
Rising, finally, into the giant head

Of tyrannosaurus, clambering past
The fist-sized brain to stare, from its eyes,
At an alleluia of swarming cars.

Solitude

Even before dawn, thoughts and prayers
are whispering from below each window
opened by a week of stifling September.
Overnight, a classmate has messaged
our fiftieth reunion batch list to observe
how the deaths of long-ago friends have
become as ordinary as war casualties,
attaching a month-old obituary scanned
from a small-town paper, *extended illness*
this time, not *suddenly*, no further reference
to the concealed carry of the body.

Yesterday, she added, I listened to a recording
of giraffes in a Viennese zoo. Though everyone
believes they are mute, they hum to each other
at night, the frequency so low nobody noticed.
For comfort, a zookeeper guessed, for reassurance,
though scientists are, for now, uncertain.

Thoughts and prayers are raising their voices,
phrases familiar as passing traffic, the closest
highway so distant, its early morning sighs
have been erased by starlings awakening,
every teeming tree chattering what sounds
like an invisible babble of surveillance.
Upstairs, two doors slam. The skylights have
been opened to crosswind, three ceiling fans
spinning as sluggishly as sermon time.
Even this early, they are helpless.

My father, once, required perfect attendance
at a church where, all summer, a funeral home
provided illustrated cardboard fans, Jesus

episodes pictured along each pew where
new hymnals, one Sunday, had been distributed,
all of them purchased to honor the memory
of somebody's loved one. Where, inside,
I found a table that listed the dates for the next
fifty years of Easter, the last embedded in an April
for which science, now, has prophesized worldwide
coastal flooding, the city in which I was reading
abandoned like a shopping mall where, after dark,
a dread of dark cars idles without headlights.

I've read that astronomers have identified
nine planets ideally positioned to observe Earth.
None of them, however, are inhabitable.
A colleague has told me she is practicing feeling
to prepare for the trauma of failing students.
She said she rehearsed for her mother's passing,
that she calculates the responses to her own death
by remembering herself in the third person,
accepting that this is what passes for comfort.
Like a planet isolated by trillions of miles
of empty darkness. Like murmurs rising through
long, steep throats until they emerge as sighs
so soft they can be translated as devotion.

The Director

1
At campus gatherings, the Director always drank white wine
    while he shook each Instructor's hand.
Except for three of us, we were all Instructors, promotion
    to assistant professor a rare reward.

At the school Christmas party, The Director said he was pleased
    that his college gave work to those who
Wouldn't be hired elsewhere. No offense, the Director said,
    and helped himself to a glass of chardonnay.

True that, as my students say, because this is a memoir
    about my first years of college teaching.
The Director constantly smiled. He showed his perfect teeth.
    Mine are crooked. I drank beer for nerves.

2
The Director had flown in the private plane of the school's
    biggest donor. He had photographs taken
Outside and inside the plane, wearing a hat sporting the donor's
    company logo when he sat in the cockpit.

I knew that because there were enlargements of five photos
    in the campus library. Under glass.
Surrounding a portrait of the donor in a tuxedo and a list
    of his accomplishments in calligraphy.

3
The Director told the athletic director, "There is only one
    Director on this campus." Yes, really.
When the intramural brochure was reprinted, there was
    an athletic coordinator. Five hundred copies

Were burned. By then, our campus had coordinators of
    facilities, faculty, and residence life.
Athletics had been overlooked like some third-world country.
    Like North Vietnam, which had just won a war.

4

During my second year, at the Founder's Day party,
    the Director asked each Instructor,
"Are you happy here?" When he got to me, his glass
    of white wine was nearly empty.

He finished it while he waited for my answer. Seriously,
    His eyes never left my face as he swallowed.
I said, "Most of the time." I gripped my bottle of local beer.
    "Interesting answer," he said. "Very."

5

The Director's gym locker was close to mine and my office mate's,
    clear enough because there was a nameplate
With his monogram embossed. "The Coordinator," we laughed,
    instead of printing it on his locker.

The Director had the locks cut and our gym clothes removed
    from our lockers because he needed room
For the school's biggest donor in our row. For a semester,
    every locker in that row stood vacant.

The athletic coordinator gave me and my office mate new locks
    and lockers. The school's biggest donor
Used the gym only very early on Sunday mornings. Or so
    we were told, having never seen him.

6

The Director declared to me that red ink could only be used
    by the Director. He referenced himself
In the third person. Yes, he did. The Director's editing
    needed to be unmistakable, he said.

The Director was funny. When he addressed us at meetings,
    he always opened with a joke to laughter.
The Director was fond of the phrase, "The sound made by
    the opening and closing of distant doors."

He used it in three speeches spaced six months apart
    so maybe no one noticed but me
And my office mate. We kept promising each other to do
    the research to see who'd said it first.

7
The Director said, "Someday, if things go well, you might
    get to fly in that private plane." Really,
He said that. He'd called me over to the library display
    and said, "You must read this list."

"Yes," I said, coughing it up like phlegm, but he was
    already waving my office mate over.
"You must read this list," I heard him say before
    I stepped behind a shelf of books.

8
The Director had the campus magazine reprinted because
    his name was misspelled. "The error is
On page one," he told the student editor. In red, he circled it
    on fifty copies to ensure reprinting.

"This is unacceptable," she quoted him, crying in my office.
    "Every name," she said, "was correct but his."
I walked her outside before I answered. My office mate and I
    no longer talked about the Director.

At least not in our office. Not in the locker room. When anyone said
    "surveillance," we held our expressions like spies.
At my fourth Christmas party, the Director said, "You've changed
    since you came on board." His skinny glass

Was empty, and he was looking for the woman who
    carried a tray of what he called flutes
That were filled with sparkling wine. "I hope so," I said.
    "Something to ponder," he said, smiling.

9

The Director wanted to be a President. His secretary leaked
    his application to a dozen colleges.
She handled all of his mailings, and she liked to tell stories.
    "Pretty soon we won't have any Directors here"

Was the joke I shared with the athletic coordinator.
    When we were off campus. When we
Couldn't stop talking about the Director, especially
    after he wasn't hired anywhere.

10

The truth is the Director sent me a letter that declared
    my employment would be terminated
After one more year of service. Remember, this is
    a memoir, so that is exactly what it said.

That plus "Since you are not tenured, you can be terminated
    without cause." The following September
The Director said, "That extra year is a gift" as he passed me
    in the hall, smiling, showing his teeth.

When the school's biggest donor visited, the Director welcomed him
    with a speech that included "The opening and
Closing of distant doors." The donor looked twenty years older than
    his library photo. He looked like his father, maybe.

11

After my grace year ended. I began to receive checks from
    the government. All I had to do for a year
Of them was admit I hadn't quit my job. That and cash
    Each one like I'd earned it.

Late summer, a school hired me. For a week I wanted to tell
        The Director face-to-face. I was worried
He'd never know, that his story about my failure was safe.
        "Stop it," my wife said, and I did,

Telling nobody at all, keeping secret I was going to direct
        a department and get a large raise.
When the contract letter arrived, it said "Department Coordinator."
        "Hilarious," I said, like a perjurer.

Consolation

While we crossed the bridge to return
from a resort island restaurant,
my friend's wife, driving slowly, said,
"Here is where the accident occurred,"
citing carelessness, inattention,
a driver texting while he veered over
the median, so much as murdering
a woman she knew well, the husband
hospitalized, severely injured,
but recovering, by now, for several months.
"Because she was driving," my friend said.
"Because, like me, he sees poorly at night."

The following morning, unannounced,
that crash survivor joined my friend and me
for golf. Introduced, I shook his hand
and carried my knowing his misery
like an extra club, even preparing,
if needed, a sentence of consolation.
For three and a half hours I believed
I was being asked to prove who I was
and became, at best, one more retiree
come south in winter and forgotten.
Afterward, over beer, I told my friend I felt
like I was spying in a changing room.

That widower, I learned the next winter,
never played another round with anyone
my friend knew, moving, by late summer,
four hundred miles to be closer to
his daughter or farther from the source
of suffering, as if distance were a way
to peace where the doors could be bolted

against the visitor who never leaves,
who does his laundry late at night and spills
cookie crumbs for which no one confesses.

My friend's wife said those in her prayers
were like refugees who had capsized
so close to shore she could see their faces,
the children unbearable, their eyes
expecting explanation to emerge
from the jabber of splash-filled screams.
She recited her verses of comfort
for the absent who had suffered loss
by violence, and though her prayer
was so familiar I could have sung it,
I stayed silent and did not declare
the old, twin pillows of humility and hope
had long ago been moved into hearsay.

Hole in the Head: A Love Poem

Performed as far back as the Stone Age, trepanning is the world's oldest surgery

1
In USA Today, back of her head
To the camera, my daughter pushes
Toward the door of a New York subway.
Six weeks after the towers tumbled, turned
Away from the lens, she's the next victim,
Her and the rest of those passengers who
Are fighting their way from explosion's smoke.

She expected the terrorists themselves
To loom out of the tunnel at the end
Of the Manhattan Bridge. "I thought," she says,
"A piece of something might open a hole
In the back of my head. All I could do
Was keep myself from falling to the floor."

2
A true story, the one about a man
Who tries to bore a tunnel through his skull,
Taking a drill to himself, twice failing
The dare of trepanning to harmony.

More truth—how his girlfriend assisted, how
She broke through, putting a hole in his head
So he overheard his brain, what sounded
Like air bubbles running under his skull.

So we marvel and shake our own sealed heads.
The girl friend records her do-it-yourself,
And there, on film, after she cuts her hair,

Her pet pigeon flutters as she opens.

Such slow, and careful, and bloody labor.
She stretches toward the lens, pinpointing
The approach, she says, of tranquility.
Though surely, I'm thinking now, we should be

Attempting self-surgery on our hearts,
Opening ourselves to longing and love,
Drilling until we look down, recording
The insistent turbulence of desire.

3
You need these things like a hole in the head,
My mother said, meaning comic books
And movies, records, extravagance.

You need these things like a hole in the head,
My father said, meaning vitamins,
More sleep, a remedy for asthma.

You need these things like a hole in the head,
My sister said, meaning boys who were
Fractured and girls with reputations.

You need these things like a hole in the head,
My teachers said, meaning cheating and
Failure, slouching, talking out of turn.

You need these things like a hole in the head,
My pastor said, meaning lust and greed,
Envy and sloth, pleasure, faithlessness.

You need these things like a hole in the head,
I told myself, meaning church and school,
Obedience, mortality, tears.

4
Three years-old, sitting on a stool for dinner, my daughter rocked herself back, then forward, then back while I managed one "stop" and one "no" before the stool toppled backwards and she was flung toward the raised stone fireplace. I lunged, too late, and saw she'd missed splitting the back of her head by less than an inch. Her skull intact, she stared up at me. For weeks, that spot a finger's width from the right angle of stone demanded my eyes down as I passed, offering terror and relief. Though years later, my student fell on a flight of stone stairs, her head snapping exactly to the edge of a step with enough force to kill her.

5
After my student died, head wounded too
Badly for repair. After her parents
Were summoned for memorial, I stood
Beside her mother in the President's
Huge house clutching a crystal flute of wine
Like a bad excuse while she let me add
Stories to sentences of sympathy.

"God bless you," I thought she murmured, the words
A tiny packet of ash, the gesture
Of grief passed like hand-written testaments
From a foreign culture, and I began
To recite my history of the dead.
I did praise and promise that ended with
Proposing her daughter's name on a prize,
The room sparkling with embellishment's light,
That girl's mother listening while looking
At me as if I were folding a flag
Like a soldier, each of us donors now,
Natal, endowing the unbearable.

6
Hundreds of ancient skulls have been discovered with circular, measured holes. What headache would drive their owners to sit for the drill? What needed to be freed? Who, surviving, would come back for more? The questions brush our hair until we touch the Braille of ourselves, feeling the breath of the ancient Peruvian man who died, every one of the seven holes in his skull showing signs of healing.

7
For weeks, my daughter refused the subway.
She walked until the aftershocks of fear
Subsided to hums of vibration. When she
Boarded again, she recognized no one
From terror's footnote. "When my head is turned,"
She said, "I feel a killer's point of view."

As if it coughs a spray of contagion,
Her anxiety plows through every crowd
Until there is no vocabulary
For security. Just below bone lies
Who she's become. Love swirls into my throat.
When I open my mouth, I moan silence,
Seeing her head like a photographer.

8
One morning, holding a drill to my skull,
I trembled. Even that brief fantasy
Of forthrightness snatched my vision naked.
I was unbalanced by held breath, shut up,
The one who required a hole in the head
To imagine happiness. Like writing
Enough lines about love that at least once
I might finish with the words heading out,
Like a space probe's miscellany, toward
The possibility of connection.

On the Eve of the Presidential Election

Seven days before this store will open,
A woman has been caught on camera
Emptying another employee's purse,
Both of them trainees for bath-oil sales,
Soap and shampoo, beautiful, thick towels.
New jobs created, the window sign says,
The shelves stocked with grand-opening prices.
In the department store next door, there are
Two aisles for toiletries, purses resting
In eleven carts I pass, cameras
Along the walls. Eighteen televisions
Show the faces of this year's candidates,
Their last-day voices muted to puzzles.
My father, one night, was robbed at gunpoint
For sixty-seven dollars, the same year
I watched a boy steal records, promising
One of them for me, desiring nothing
In return but my knowing "Party Doll"
Had come for free. "There's the atom bomb now,"
He said, "no sense waiting for what we want."

Today a woman showed me my borough
On a screen centered upon her steel desk.
She zoomed to my street, enlarging my house
Until I was afraid my wife would walk
Outside to the long-term consequences
Of cameras. Suddenly, my address
Looked so much a target I was nearly
Afraid to drive home. A candidate's name
Circled the violet mug she sipped from.
When she said, "I can't stop looking," her voice
Was full of launch codes. The widespread weapons
That may murder us have been diminished

To mortgages and stocks and credit cards.
Tomorrow half of these shoppers will not vote.
I know a man, now, who pretends to be
A customer, searching for shoplifters.
Soon terrible thoughts will be photographed.

Faith

> As late as 1892, in Vermont, the body of Mercy Brown, thought to be a vampire, was exhumed for public autopsy.
> —The Smithsonian

Mercy's Father
This story begins once upon a dark, ignorant time
seductive with unhappiness as if ruin were
a handsome prince. A father watches his neighbors pry
his daughter out of her months-old grave to prove
her vampire's heart is uncorrupted. What's more, that heart,
in ashes, will cure consumption victims, his son Edwin
and whoever else has a persistent, bloody cough.

My Neighbor's Father
On the anniversary of success,
a neighbor's father watches a video
of his heart surgery. Four years now,
and because he cannot see his face
or even his body beyond the cavity
created for repair, it's not traumatic
to see himself opened and dead,
invaded by instruments. He says
he is seventy, hopes to watch his heart
for twenty years. That video begins
mid-operation and ends before closing,
a sampler, he says, as if his heart
was one among assorted candies.

My Father
Crying, a traditional song passed down
by mothers. Silence, a simple box step
of fathers who cannot use its rhythm
for anything but the lurch and shuffle.

The chorus with its hint of forgiveness,
my mother humming that song through her last
crossword puzzle, her last letter to me,
the one my father, between football games,
walked to the mailbox because the forecast
promised overnight snow, nodding to her
his ballad of silence as her failed heart
permitted the small, private grace to dress
for bed before she lay down for dying.

For fifty years, my father shook his head
to dancing. He sat and waited, nervous
as a patient's friend. My mother long dead,
he found ways to say what cannot be said,
putting on his bolo tie, polishing
his shoes, and repeating, from memory,
my poem about her death, reciting
while I ate the breakfasts he made, sweet rolls
and sausages, as if recollecting
had turned so specialized he could perfect
only small things. His kitchen was orange;
the oven was broken; a penciled sign
above it said, "Turn Off." He spoke my lines
like a prerecorded message, and then
he hung up and bowed his head to eating.

Mercy's Father
This story continues with Edwin agreeing
to devour the ashes of his sister's heart--
with his father looking on and listening
to the sky for anything in return--
with God's silence swirling the clouds like ashes
as He passed over like a distant tradition.

My Neighbor's Father
If he could find a rotary phone, he tells me,
he could dial the long nines to his wife's voice
breathless from her downstairs hurry and failing heart.

He's seven years alone, three weeks sleepless.
By now, his house has learned a language
he cannot translate. All morning it's chanted
the vowels of threat and fear. By noon the rooms
darkened for rain. Light fled to where everlasting
breathes promises. On the kitchen table, papers
and books, the small, reusable place setting.
The heart of a king, he's read, was mummified
with mint and myrtle, frankincense and daisy.
After centuries, it's a curiosity
that travels like a campaigner. In each room,
the evening waits like a woman he's paid for.

My Father
The face of Christ has surfaced
On the inside of the door
To my father's garage where
His car has been gone three years,
Sold and replaced with wishing.
Only the neighbor who has
Been hired to cut grass enters,
Raising and lowering
The door from the outside.
My father, if he returned
To driving, would know miracle.
My father, if he could slip
His shoes on over ulcers,
Might reaffirm promise.
His knees with no cartilage
Play the bone on bone etudes
Of pain; his pacemaker keeps
One thing tuned in his body.
The face of Christ has waited,
Now, for two and a half years.
The lawn boy has traded
My father's tools for dope, the theft
As secret as revelation.
I sit beside my father

And his elevated legs.
Nothing in his living room
Shows a face, not my mother,
Twenty-one years dead, not me
Or my sister or my daughter
Become, this year, the age
Of Christ when he preached and died.
In his bedroom all of us wait,
Like Christ, to be witnessed,
But here, his feet wrapped in gauze,
My father holds out a picture
Of himself at eighteen, asking,
"Do you believe it's me?"
And because he refuses
To tilt that picture up, I kneel
Beside his chair to say "Yes,"
My father keeping that picture
Faced my way so long, I say "Yes"
Again to ensure he's heard me.

Mercy's Father
This story ends as Mercy's father packs her things,
the quilt she'd stitched from scraps and remnants
to tuck under the chins of children whose hearts
would have beaten in a room that shimmered
like safety and longevity. Her heart of soot is
so powerful, he touches her clothes, imagines
her longing for a lover's breath buried between
her frantic breasts that lift to his tongue and teeth
as if she wished him to devour her cursed heart.

My Neighbor's Father
Listen, he says, Natalie Adler
had eyes that suddenly closed
and could not be opened
for three days, so regular,
that habit, she could have been
sent from God to remind us

about how faith is tested before
the re-emergence of light.
He is excited about intimations
of paradise, one we can believe in
because it can be measured
in days, because our privacies
are witnessed, because our choices
earn what we deserve. Think, he says,
about three days of darkness
that passes all understanding
and thereafter lifts like eyelids.

My Father
After his surgery, my father feels
for his pulse, saying "still there"
on the quarter hour like a chorus
from a hymn played by the carillon
from the nearby Catholic church.
And though he believes his heart
will soon be unnecessary in a world
without gravity or sorrow, he listens
and counts, gauging the tempo.
Sixty-six, he says as if he's in training.
Sixty-eight, stopping to expose,
for the second time, his bypass scar.
"Still there," he says, as if he needs
to coax a heartbeat with prayer.

Even when he stops watching
television, when he sleeps twelve hours
a day and naps three times,
his fingers go to his wrist
as he wakes and says, "Still there,"
giving in to the walker,
acquiescing to the wheelchair,
half his weight vanished although
he eats, as always, everything
that is served, Even when his sentences

grow shorter, the ends lost like addresses,
phone numbers, and names,
his fingers return to his wrist
for the braille of "still there,"
looking down at the carpet
while I wait, so quiet,
holding my breath until he speaks.

The Invention of Worship

Now we are told that cave paintings
in Europe depict, not animals,
but constellations. That there was,
from prehistory, metaphorical
portraiture of the distant.

Consider the high risk for night scenes,
sacrifice, sometimes, to eyewitness
where the ceiling of the world had been
decorated by gods so generous
they displayed an encyclopedia
of their dreams, every pin prick of light
with purpose, something more than beasts
waiting to be discovered by daring
the clawed that controlled darkness.

The future was as unformed as
heaven, a wish in need of language.
Idea, not yet named, had been born,
a shape evoked in unreliable light.
A chant, at last, rose from others
in a smoke-choked cave, a syllable
repeated with the lilt of approval,
the early syllable for awe.

Though such comfort, after all,
was everywhere elusive, the land
violent and cruel, so little
to be done about suffering despite
spears and clubs readied nearby,
whatever else might be said lost
in eviction or death, that gallery
given over, as it often is, to brutes.

Acknowledgements

These poems, sometimes in a different form, were published by the following journals:

"Fimbulwinter," *The Gettysburg Review*
"After the Election, Traditional Forms ," *Lake Effect*
"Symmetry," *The Southern Review*
"Isolation," *World Literature Today*
"The Beheaded," *Alaska Quarterly Review*
"In the Era of Collective Thought," *Zingara Poetry Review*
"Contagious," *Gargoyle*
"The Mussolini Diaries," *American Journal of Poetry*
"Soeur Sourire and the Vanishing of Nuns," *One*
"The Drowning of W.C. Fields ," *One*
"How Silly Grew," *One*
"The Museum of American Tragedy," *GW Review*
"The Director," *River Styx*
"Consolation," *Innisfree*
"Hole in the Head," *Barrow Street*
"On the Eve of the Presidential Election," *St. Ann's Review*
"Faith," *American Journal of Poetry*
"The Magician's Son," *The Associative Press*
"Perspective," *Proem*
"After the Election News, Human Subjects," *American Journal of Poetry*

"The Beheaded" was reprinted by *Verse Daily*

Gary Fincke's latest collection of poems, *The Infinity Room*, won the Wheelbarrow Books Prize for Established Poets (Michigan State, 2019). Winner of Poetry Magazine's Bess Hokin Prize, two Pushcart Prizes, and Ohio State's Wheeler Prize, he has published fourteen collections of poetry. His fiction and nonfiction collections have won the Flannery O'Connor Prize for Short Fiction and the Robert C. Jones Prize for Short Prose. He recently retired after founding and then directing the Writers Institute at Susquehanna University for decades.

www.ingramcontent.com/pod-product-compliance
Lightning Source LLC
Chambersburg PA
CBHW022008120526
44592CB00034B/746